In memory of Oscar Jeschie Rosen and Rachel Rosen
(née Kesler), who were on the same train, Convoy 62
MR

For my dear friend Simmy
BP

With thanks to Andy Pearce at the
UCL Centre for Holocaust Education

First US edition 2025
First published by Walker Books Ltd. (UK) 2025

Library of Congress Catalog Card Number pending
ISBN 978-1-5362-3894-5

24 25 26 27 28 29 CCP 10 9 8 7 6 5 4 3 2 1

Printed in Shenzhen, Guangdong, China

This book was typeset in Bookman.
The illustrations were done in ink, charcoal, and pencil.

Candlewick Studio
an imprint of
Candlewick Press
99 Dover Street
Somerville, Massachusetts 02144

www.candlewickstudio.com

ONE DAY

A TRUE STORY OF SURVIVAL
IN THE HOLOCAUST

ILLUSTRATED BY

MICHAEL ROSEN   BENJAMIN PHILLIPS

CANDLEWICK STUDIO

an imprint of Candlewick Press

ONE DAY our lives changed.

We didn't think about yesterday

and tomorrow may not happen.

We had to cope with what was in front of us

on that one day.

Get through one day

and then on to the next.

One day at a time.

One day after another.

We were Hungarian Jews, living in an area called the Marais in Paris.

We were Communists in the Resistance.

This meant we were in hiding.

We were fighting the Nazis.

And the Nazis were hunting down Jews.

Jews like us.

We had false papers, which were about to run out; we had to pick up

the new ones from our old home in the Marais.

But my father and I were spotted.

We were followed

and we got picked off.

It was December 28, 1942.

This one day changed everything.

We were no longer free to fight the Nazis.

We were arrested by the French police and handed over to the Nazis.

We were interrogated.

That meant we were beaten. Then we were sent to the Compiègne camp.

We had hardly anything to eat—a little ball of bread a day.

We were in this camp for two months, breaking stones.

I was just skin and bone.

Get through one day and then on to the next.

One day at a time. One day after another.

Then we were transferred to the camp at Drancy.

This was a new housing complex that had been turned into a prison camp for Jews.

Jews were being deported day by day. We didn't know where.

All that we knew was that they didn't come back.

We called the place they were deporting people to "Pitchipoï."

We said over and over, "We're not going to Pitchipoï."

We came up with the idea of digging a tunnel—to escape.

We started on September 15, 1943.

One day that changed our lives.

Get through one day and then on to the next.

One day at a time. One day after another.

There was Maurice, René, Georges, Roger,
Abraham, Claude, and myself on the core team.
Starting out in a cellar under one of the blocks of apartments.

Digging, lining the tunnel,
packing the earth down in the cellars.
In the end, there were more than forty of us taking turns.

The tunnel was four feet high, less than three feet wide. Can you imagine that?
We got lights down there and propped up the tunnel with wood.

It was tough, what with the heat and the lack of air . . . We had to go up to
the ground above to check that we were going in the right direction.

Even my dad was on the team.

Some of us fainted on the job.

Get through one day and then on to the next.

One day at a time. One day after another.

By November, the tunnel was over 115 feet long.

Not far to go—maybe eight feet, or twelve.

But then, with hardly any more tunnel to dig,

one of our guys heard the Nazis talking about a tunnel.

Those of us down there had to get out fast.

Get out! Get out!

When we came out of the tunnel into the cellar,
we just dumped our clothes and ran.
We thought we had gotten away with it.
But the Nazis found the entrance to the tunnel
in the cellar.

They found the pile of dirty clothes,
and there was a pair of trousers
with wrapping paper in the pocket.
On the paper, a name.

This one day changed everything.

We would no longer be able
to dig our way to freedom.
We knew that they would put us
on one of the trains to Pitchipoï.

They arrested this guy whose name was on the wrapping paper,
and they started to interrogate him.

To start off with, he said nothing.
But then they did their usual:
they said they would punish many
innocent people because of one man.
That would mean women and
children being locked in
cellars with no food.
So this guy gave them
thirteen names.
He made sure it was men
who had no children
in the camp.

I was one of them. And my father.

We were taken to a cellar and beaten.

They asked us to face the wall and they set up a mock execution.

We admitted we were the ones who dug the tunnel.

They thanked us for having talked about the tunnel.

"You won't be shot. We'll deport you."

We talked about escaping again,
but we couldn't get out.

NOUS N'IRONS PAS À PITCHIPOÏ

Next we were taken to a train at Bobigny station in Paris.

This was a train made up of cattle trucks.

Twelve hundred Jews were put into these trucks.

Men, women, and children.

There was crying and screaming.

We found out later that this was Convoy 62.

It left Bobigny station on November 20, 1943.

One day.

A day that would change everything

for nearly everyone on board that train.

We didn't know anything about the Holocaust then.

All we knew was that something bad was going on, something wrong.

We were going on a journey and not coming back

unless we did something about it.

One of the guys in the Resistance had heard that the train would slow down in a tunnel at a place called Bar-le-Duc. We'd hidden tools in our clothes.

On the train people were packed into the trucks.
No food.
No toilets.
Not knowing where they were going.
There was crying and screaming.
And the smell was terrible.

We got to work on the bars in our truck. But they wouldn't budge.

Luckily, there were two strong rugby players with us,

Roger and Georges. They tore the bars off.

When the train slowed down, my dad jumped.

And then we jumped!

We ran back to find my father, but he wasn't there.

But we knew the rule of the Resistance: whoever can get away

mustn't worry about the others. So that's what we did.

This one day . . .

We got to Bar-le-Duc railway station, but there were Nazi guards along the platforms.

But we also saw that there was a mixed bunch of people standing about there—forced laborers, deportees—and we mingled among them, unnoticed.

We had a fifty-franc note on us,
and we bought tickets back to Paris.

What about Dad?

When he jumped, he hit the roof of the tunnel and passed out.

When he woke up, he realized he had to run . . .

He got to a farmhouse and the couple living there took him in.

They bathed his wound and hid him.

When the Nazis came looking for him, the couple said they knew nothing.

I often think about that.

If the Nazis had found my dad, they would have shot that couple.

I've never forgotten them. Monsieur and Madame Médard.

Then in the morning one of them took him to Paris.

And I met up with him.

Can you imagine that? I thought I had lost him.
I thought that on that one day he was gone,
and I'd never see him again.
And here he was.

We hugged each other like we had never hugged each other before.

We asked each other,
where was the train going?

We didn't know.

And then we went back to join the Resistance
to fight the Nazis.
And that's a true story.
My name is Eugène Handschuh.
And my father—
may his memory be for a blessing—
was Oscar.

You may ask, where did the train go?

What happened to the twelve hundred people on that train?

There were nineteen of us who jumped
on that one day.

The rest went to Auschwitz.

Only twenty-nine came back.

And that's a true story.

Remember:

Get through one day and then on to the next.

One day at a time. One day after another.

AUTHOR'S NOTE

It's very difficult to find any hope in the horror and catastrophe of the Holocaust. Even so, here and there, we hear of stories where people were able to help each other or escape, and it can give us a lift.

I read about this story because I was researching what happened to my father's uncle and aunt in France. As you've seen, there is a prison camp in the story—my father's uncle and aunt were in that camp at the same time as the people in this story. And there's a train—a "convoy"—that deported Jews from Paris to Auschwitz. My father's uncle and aunt were on that very same train. They didn't come back.

The story as I tell it here is in the voice of Eugène Handschuh. It's based on interviews he gave in the press (e.g., in *Libération*) and also a book called *Nous n'irons pas à Pitchipoï: Le tunnel du camp de Drancy* by Janet Thorpe (2004, Éditions de Fallois). It is not, however, an exact retelling of real events—for instance, I have not included Eugène's brother Louis in this story. Louis was also at Drancy and escaped the convoy.

When the deportations from France to the concentration and extermination camps started happening, people in France didn't know where the people being deported were going or what was happening to them. They made up a nonsense word for the place or places where people were going—"Pitchipoï." It wasn't long before people in France realized that the people on the deportation trains (the convoys) weren't coming back and it was almost impossible to get any news of where they were or what was happening to them. We often think of nonsense as meaning "funny," but sometimes it can mean "absurd," and this absurd language becomes a way of coping with the horror of what is unknown and yet terrible.

Throughout the story, I use the phrase "one day." That's because the piece was largely written for the 2022 commemoration of Holocaust Memorial Day, which chose the phrase as its motto for that year.

Thanks to Professor Helen Weinstein from Historyworks, who commissioned me to write this piece.